GOING

LIVE

Six tracks about living for God

Contributors :

Terry Dunnell
Andrew Graystone
Chris Powell

Scripture Union
130 City Road, London, EC1V 2NJ

Serendipity UK
48 Peterborough Road, London, SW6 3EB

In this series....

Going live   —   Living for God   (ISBN 0 86201 668 1)

Tuned in   —   Knowing God   (ISBN 0 86201 670 3)

Sounds like me   —   Am I OK?   (ISBN 0 86201 665 7)

Making contact   —   Living with others   (ISBN 0 86201 666 5)

System breakdown   —   What's gone wrong?   (ISBN 0 86201 669 X)

Power supply   —   Power for good – power for evil   (ISBN 0 86201 667 3)

© Serendipity UK 1990
First published 1990
ISBN 0 86201 668 1

British Library Cataloguing in Publication Data
Dunnell, Terry
   Going live: living for God.
   1. Young people. Christian life
   I. Title II. Graystone, Andrew III. Powell,
Chris IV. Series
   248.83

All Bible quotations, except where otherwise stated,
are from the Good News Bible – Old Testament:
Copyright © American Bible Society 1976; New
Testament: Copyright © American Bible Society
1966, 1971, 1976.

Printed by Ebenezer Baylis and Son Limited,
The Trinity Press, Worcester and London.

Acknowledgements
Cover design and artwork: Adept Design.
Internal artwork: Pauline Adams.
Series editor: Andrew Graystone.
The prayer on page 9 is from **The Alternative Service
Book 1980** and is used with permission.
The rap on page 43 is by Peter Graystone and is from
Learning All Together.
Photographs by Gordon Gray

Contents

Instructions

 means do this bit by yourself.

 means choose a partner and work together.

 means discuss this with the whole group.

Before you start...

Before using one of the tracks in this book, read the notes on page 44 and the advice on specific tracks on pages 46 to 48.

What's most

Pete was the first home. Dad had left a note saying there were two pieces of chocolate gateau in the fridge – one for him, one for his sister Chris.

He had eaten his piece, and picked up and licked up all the loose bits on the plate, but Chris's piece of sticky-scrumptious, absolutely wicked, triple-decker, fresh-cream, real-chocolate chocolate gateau was still staring at him defiantly through the open fridge door.

'Go on,' he told himself. 'It's not a sin to be greedy – it's not like stealing – well, it is stealing, but it's not a real sin like... like... mass-murder. Everyone's got their weak points : Tony's always telling lies, Ian always hands work in late, and Dad even cleans his ears out in public. Compared to them a bit of pigging hardly counts. I can't help having a weak spot for chocolate....

Anyway, Chris is fat enough and she's got more spots than you could pop in a month – well she hasn't, but she would have if she ate this. So I'm doing her a favour really....'

So he disposed of the second piece of gateau. It was just a shame he forgot to dispose of the note as well, before Chris got home....

mportant to me?

 GROUP Pete said he couldn't help it. Take a vote to see who thinks he could and who thinks he couldn't. Why?

 SOLO Finish this cartoon, showing what happens next....

 TWOS What would be the best way to keep someone else's gateau safe from Pete? Draw or describe a way.

TWOS Pete had a weakness for chocolate cake. Think of one thing that you like a lot. Choose something that you would find it very hard to give up. Write it here...

....

...then tell your partner about it.

Find out what it would take to persuade your partner to give up the thing he or she has written above. For instance, if they have written 'chocolate' you might say 'Would you give up chocolate for £100...£500...£1000?' Or else you might say, 'Would you give up chocolate if you found out it killed brain cells?' or, 'Would you give up chocolate if it gave you terrible spots?' Be as imaginative as you can. Try to find out just how much they like it!

■STOP■

What does God have to say about our priorities?

- ■ Read the Bible passages.
- ■ Mark any discoveries you make.
- ■ Jot down any questions you are left with.
- ■ Talk about your discoveries and questions with the group.....

What did the disciples 'lose' because they followed Jesus?

▶PLAY▶

Jesus taught that we should forget our own hopes and wants. Instead we should 'follow him' and let him take control of our lives.

What would the disciples have thought when Jesus said they had to 'carry a cross'?

THEN Jesus called the crowd and his disciples to him. 'If anyone wants to come with me,' he told them, 'he must forget self, carry his cross, and follow me. For whoever wants to save his own life will lose it; but whoever loses his life for me and for the gospel will save it. Does a person win anything if he gains the whole world but loses his life? Of course not! There is nothing he can give to regain his life. If a person is ashamed of me and of my teaching in this godless and wicked day, then the Son of Man will be ashamed of him when he comes in the glory of his Father with the holy angels.'

Mark 8:34–38

As Jesus was starting on his way again, a man ran up, knelt before him, and asked him, 'Good Teacher, what must I do to receive eternal life?'

'Why do you call me good?' Jesus asked him. 'No one is good except God alone. You know the commandments: "Do not commit murder ; do not commit adultery; do not steal; do not accuse anyone falsely; do not cheat; respect your father and your mother."'

'Teacher,' the man said, 'ever since I was young, I have obeyed all these commandments.'

Jesus looked straight at him with love and said, 'You need only one thing. Go and sell all you have and give the money to the poor, and you will have riches in heaven; then come and follow me.' When the man heard this, gloom spread over his face, and he went away sad, because he was very rich.

Mark 10:17–22

What does it mean to 'follow' someone?

▶PLAY

This man had been pretty good. Why wasn't that enough for Jesus?

Why did Jesus ask the man to do this?

Why was he so sad?

FASE FORWARD

Finish one of these sentences.

SOLO
The rich young man who Jesus met is...

...not at all like me because.....

....

...a bit like me because...

....

...a lot like me because...

....

SOLO
The thought of giving up everything to follow Jesus makes me feel.....

Secure ❏   Out of control ❏
Threatened ❏   Happy ❏
Unsure ❏   Privileged ❏
Resentful ❏   Other.....................

SOLO
How closely are you following Jesus? Or are you walking in the opposite direction? Draw yourself somewhere on this path.

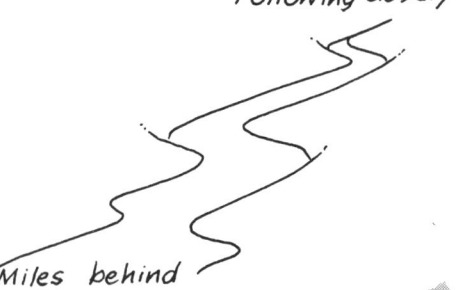

Following closely

Miles behind

GROUP
Jesus said that anyone who follows him will have to 'carry their cross'. Part of what this means is that it will sometimes be hard to follow him. Think of situations which you know in which it would be hard to follow Jesus. Talk about them.

TWOS
I could follow Jesus better if the other members of this group would....(Tick one or more.)

Pray for me regularly   ❏
Go around with me all the time   ❏
Get off my back and leave me in peace   ❏
Get to know me better   ❏

Other ....

Other ....

WHAT WILL YOU DO?

In some countries of the world Christians are imprisoned and even killed for their beliefs. Imagine that a law has been introduced in this country banning all Christian meetings. What will you do?

Collection

Take up a 'collection' in the group by passing round a bag. But instead of putting money in the bag, write or draw what you would like to offer to God. It could be a sum of money to be given to someone in need, or it could be an offering of time. You may decide that you ought to be more ready to share some of your possessions....in which case you could write or draw that intention and put it in the collection. Give a few moments for group members to think about their offering, then pass the collection bag in silence. The offerings are just between God and the giver, so someone should be appointed to destroy them without looking at them.

Prayer

You could say this prayer together.

Yours, Lord is the greatness, the power,
the glory, the splendour and the
majesty;
for everything in heaven
and on earth is yours.
All things come from you,
and of your own do we give you.
Amen.

TOUGH TALKING

Is it wrong for Christians to be rich? Do you think it's harder to be a Christian if you have a lot of money and possessions?

Once you have committed your life completely to God, is it possible to change your mind and stop being a Christian?

GOING FURTHER

If you want to think more about following Jesus check out these Bible passages:

Luke 9:57–62 – All or nothing
Luke 19:1–10 – A tax man follows Jesus
Philippians 3:8–14

–Paul follows Jesus

Who's ir

LOAD

Steve dashed into 'Burger– U– Scoff' and collapsed into the seat next to Imran. He was an hour late. On the table were two burgers, ordered an hour earlier. They were curling unhappily at the edges.

'Where have you been?' demanded Imran.

'It's been one of those days,' Steve said. 'I forgot to set my alarm, so I didn't have time for breakfast. I had a close-up demonstration of the new braking system on a BMW while I was running for the bus. Lunchtime I dashed into town for the new 'Frantic Pose' album, but they'd sold out. And if that stupid old bag hadn't got in the way I might have got back to school on time. The eggs she was carrying splattered my trousers. Then when I got home I argued with Mum because she made me walk the dog and I had to drag the mangy, flea ridden mutt past every single lamp-post.'

'So you upset a BMW driver, an old lady, a box of eggs, your mum and your dog all in one day. And to cap it all you let these burgers curl up and die.'

'It's just not my lucky day. Couldn't be helped. There was nothing I could do!' Steve said, adding 'Oh no...' as his elbow caught Imran's coke and spread it evenly across his shirt, his trousers and his slippers.

'Slippers! What am I wearing slippers for? Must have forgotten to change them when I came out.'

control?

 Why do you think Steve had such a terrible day? (Tick one of these answers or invent your own.)

His bio-rhythms were against him ❏
God planned it to teach him patience ❏
He got out of bed the wrong side ❏
He forgot to read his horoscope ❏
It was just one of those unlucky days ❏
The Devil was trying to mess up his day ❏

Other ....

 Compare your answers to see what the group thought was most responsible for Steve's terrible day, and what was least responsible.

 Have you ever had a day when nothing went right? Tell the group about it.

 How much do you agree with each of the following statements?

SA = Strongly agree
TA = Tend to agree
TD = Tend to disagree
SD = Strongly disagree

The world is remote-controlled by God like a toy aeroplane
SA   TA   TD   SD

Every human being is in control of their own life
SA   TA   TD   SD

God thinks he controls the world, but really the Devil does
SA   TA   TD   SD

The world is out of control
SA   TA   TD   SD

The world is not ordered by God, or by humans, but by sheer luck
SA   TA   TD   SD

STOP

What does God have to say about who rules the world?

- Read the Bible passages.
- Mark any discoveries you make.
- Jot down any questions you are left with.
- Talk about your discoveries and questions with the group.....

PLAY

This passage is part of the story of Job from the Old Testament. In it the Devil (or Satan) challenges God to see who is really in control of the world. God lets the Devil test Job's loyalty.

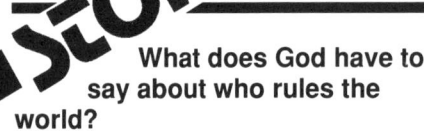

Why did God let the Devil test Job?
Can the Devil only do what God allows him to?

WHEN the day came for the heavenly beings to appear before the LORD, Satan was there among them. The LORD asked him, 'What have you been doing?'

Satan answered, 'I have been walking here and there, roaming round the earth.'

'Did you notice my servant Job?' the LORD asked. 'There is no one on earth as faithful and good as he is. He worships me and is careful not to do anything evil.'

Satan replied, 'Would Job worship you if he got nothing out of it? You have always protected him and his family and everything he owns. You bless everything he does, and you have given him enough cattle to fill the whole country. But now suppose you take away everything he has – he will curse you to your face!'

'All right,' the LORD said to Satan, 'everything he has is in your power, but you must not hurt Job himself.' So Satan left.

Job 1:6–12

What is the 'armour' God gives us, and how can it be 'put on'?

BUILD up your strength in union with the LORD and by means of his mighty power. Put on all the armour that God gives you, so that you will be able to stand up against the Devil's evil tricks. For we are not fighting against human beings but against the wicked spiritual forces in the heavenly world, the rulers, authorities, and cosmic powers of this dark age.

Ephesians 6:10–12

Paul wrote this advice to the Christians in Ephesus.

What 'enemy' are Christians fighting against?

SINCE the children, as he calls them, are people of flesh and blood, Jesus himself became like them and shared their human nature. He did this so that through his death he might destroy the Devil, who has the power over death, and in this way set free those who were slaves all their lives because of their fear of death.

Hebrews 2:14–15

This passage from the letter to the Hebrew Christians talks about how Jesus beat the Devil by living and dying as a human being.

What made Jesus' death so special? How come it destroyed the Devil?

FAST FORWARD

After reading those passages, what answer do you think the Bible gives to the question: 'Who's in control of the world?' Mark any answers you think are false, or add your own answer.

The Devil is in control and everything that goes wrong is his fault. ....

No one. The world is out of control. ....

God has total power, but he allows the Devil some control for now. ....

Everything is guided by fate, and everything that will ever happen is already programmed in. ....

....

....

Read through this passage and cross out the things that the Bible *does not* say about the Devil. Leave all the things that the Bible *does* say about the Devil.

The Devil really does exist. He has horns and a tail and carries a pitch-fork. He is an enemy to God and tries to trick human beings. He lives in a fiery place called hell. In fact he is a bit of a joke. He is very powerful. God lets the Devil have some power for now. The Devil is as strong as God. One day he may destroy God altogether. He has been beaten by Jesus, so there's no need to be afraid of death any more. If you keep on the right side of him the Devil will help you out.

List two ways in which you can see the Devil's 'evil tricks' at work in the world.

1 ....

2...

What 'evil tricks' do you think the Devil would like to get up to in this group? How could he try to spoil it?

1 ....

2...

What could you do to stand up against these evil tricks'? What 'armour' could you use to defend yourselves?

1 ....

....

2...

....

Which of these pictures do you think best describes the way God treats the world? He is...

...like an owner controlling a dog

...like a skilled general leading an army in battle

...like a mother teaching a child to walk

...like a company director managing a business

IIPAUSEII

...like a pilot flying an aeroplane
...like a manager coaching a sports team
...like a teacher controlling a class
...your own description

Share your answer with the group and say why you chose the answer you did.

WHAT WILL YOU DO?

Your best friend agrees to meet you in the burger bar, then keeps you waiting for an hour. He or she eventually arrives and just says, 'It couldn't be helped. My horoscope said I'd be upsetting people all day.' What will you do?

TOUGH TALKING

When things go wrong is it always the Devil's fault, or do some things 'just happen'? Is there such a thing as fate or luck?

Some people read their horoscopes or play with ouija boards to try to find out what will happen to them. Why do you think they do this? Is it OK?

TWOS Think of one situation in the whole world, one situation in your own country, and one situation in your own life, where you would like to see God's control more clearly. Pray together, either silently or out loud, asking God to take control. Ask him how you can be part of that too.

GROUP **Either** sing a song about God being in control of the world, such as 'Jesus is Lord, creation's voice proclaims it' or 'For this purpose Christ was revealed'

or write a chant or rap on a large sheet of paper that has the words 'We know for sure that God's in control' as every second line.

eg
When things go wrong and we can't cope.
We know for sure that God's in control.
The world's getting worse but we've got hope,
We know for sure that God's in control.

GOING FURTHER

If you want to think more about who rules the world, check out these Bible passages:
Psalm 8   –Our place in God's plan
Hebrews 2:5– 9   –Jesus in control
Ephesians 1:21– 22 –Jesus over all

Ideas for

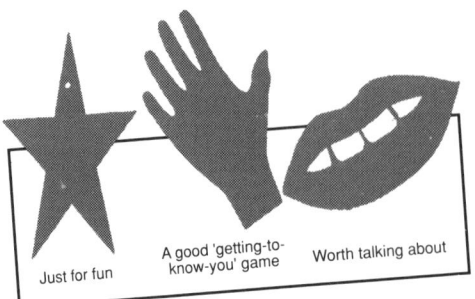

Just for fun | A good 'getting-to-know-you' game | Worth talking about

The hello game

Before you meet, someone from the group will need to prepare a set of cards – about three for each person in the group. Each card has an instruction on it including the name of a group member. Make sure that everyone's name is included, and take out the cards that mention people who haven't come to the group. The instructions might be, for instance: Blow a kiss to Mary, Shake your fist at Tom, Comb Ali's hair, Undo a button on Bill's shirt.

Sit in a circle and put the cards face down in the centre. Everyone takes a card in turn and does whatever it says. Other group members should give lots of help and encouragement, especially if you can't remember each other's names.

If you're feeling too shy to do this individually, you could all take a card and then do the action at the same time. Then shuffle the cards and try again.

Clumps

You need one person to act as 'caller' for this game. The caller calls out a number between one and ten (or one and six if the group is small, and everyone else tries to link arms in a clump (group) with that number of people. Then the caller calls

another number, and again everyone tries to link arms with that number. Each time there will be a few people who don't make it. Include them in the next round.

For a variation, you could play 'Threes'. This time the aim is always to get into clumps of three, and instead of calling out a number, the caller calls out a category such as 'People wearing something blue' or 'People wearing a watch'. Everyone tries to get into a clump of three people who fit that description.

Or you could try 'Silent clumps', or even 'Clumps with your eyes closed'!

Don't forget to swap callers from time to time so everyone can join in!

Musical chairs (with a difference!)

Everyone knows how to play musical chairs. But try this for a variation. Put out a circle of stable chairs facing outwards. You need the same number of chairs as you have players. Everyone walks round the room to the music, touching each wall in turn. When the music stops everyone tries to find a chair to sit on. For the second round take a chair or two away and so on. The difference is that in this version of the game no one drops out. If you can't find a chair to sit on, just sit on someone's lap. As the chairs get fewer and fewer more and more people will have to sit on each other's laps. Keep going till there is only one (very strong) chair and everyone is sitting on it!

Electric fence

You'll need between five and ten people for this exercise. If there are more of you, split into two or more teams.

your group

Make an 'electric fence' by tying a piece of string or a washing line across the room about a metre above the ground. You could tie it between two high-backed chairs. Give the team a rolled-up blanket to represent an injured person.

Everybody stands on one side of the fence. The task is to get the whole team, and the injured person, over the electric fence without touching it. You can't use any other funiture or equipment to help – just yourselves. It's a good test of teamwork.

Dodgems

Everybody stands in a circle facing inwards. On the word 'go' everybody simply has to move across the circle to the opposite side without touching anybody else in the process. A very simple idea, but quite hard to do! Try it slowly at first. Then try doing it without speaking at all. Then for a real challenge, try doing it with your eyes closed.

Killer wink

Everyone sits in a circle on the floor facing inwards. Now choose one person to be the 'catcher' and send them out of the room, while the rest of you select one person to be the 'killer'. When the catcher comes back into the room he or she stands in the middle of the circle. The catcher's job is to work out who the killer is. Meanwhile the killer 'kills' as many members of the group as he can by secretly winking at them. If the killer winks at you you have to die in a loud and dramatic fashion ! See how many people are finished off before the catcher works out who the killer is.

All together now !

How often do you get the chance to spend an evening with the older members of your church? In lots of churches, adults and children and young people hardly ever get together. No wonder they hardly know each other.

Why not organise an activity that everyone can join in, from the youngest to the oldest? Here are a few tried and tested ideas....

■ Splash out and hire the local swimming pool for an evening.

■ Put on a variety concert or talent show.

■ Try a camera quiz. Lend each group a camera and give them a list of zany things to photograph, eg the whole group in a phone box.

■ Hire a band or borrow some records for a barn dance-cum-disco. Try to include some music from every generation.

■ Go carol singing together.

How can I get

LOAD

Saturday morning. Ten o'-clock. Me and the others met up outside the swimming pool. No Dawn.

'She's always late,' said Simon.

Now that's not very fair, 'cos Dawn's usually pretty punctual. But these last few weeks she seems to have been slipping away from our group. Dunno why. She just doesn't seem interested anymore. Anyway, while the others went and changed I gave her a ring.

'What's up Dawn? Overslept?'

'No. I just didn't feel like it. Too much to do.'

'Too bad. It seems like ever since you've been going out with Gary you've had no time for the rest of us. We never see you at church or Christian Union or anything.'

'Yeah, maybe. I guess I've put God on standby for the moment. To be honest he feels a million miles away just now. I used to think that God spoke to me, but now I'm not interested in him. And with the way things are I don't suppose he's interested in me either.'

We said our goodbyes and I went off to the pool.

Twenty minutes later Dawn swam past me in the deep end.

'Hey...what are you doing here?'

'What does it look like....the hundred meters hurdles?'

'I thought you were supposed to be too busy.'

'Yeah....well I figured I could spare the time. Anyway it's ages since I've been swimming with you lot. I sort of miss you. Maybe God's trying to tell me something.'

closer to Jesus?

 What do you think God might be wanting to tell Dawn? Write it in this space.

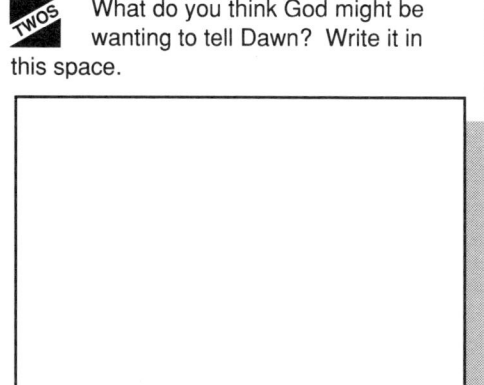

 Have you ever felt that God was 'speaking' to you? How did he speak? What happened? Tell the rest of the group about it.

Jesus said we must 'listen to his words' and obey him. Look at the list below. Try to agree on the three best ways your group could hear what Jesus has to say.

Listen to sermons   .....
Read Christian books   .....
Read the Bible by yourselves   .....
Sit in silence and ask Jesus to
     speak to you   .....
Study the Bible together   .....
Share your own ideas about life   .....
Watch religious programmes on TV   .....

Other ....

 Which of these endings would you use to finish this sentence? Cross out the ones you think are not right, and add any others you can think of.

A person who is close to Jesus....

...is always smiling
...spends time listening to God
...carries a Bible everywhere
...attracts other people to God
...prays a lot
...has all the latest Christian tapes
...shows love to other people
...obeys God's commands

Other...

 Think back to this time last year. Would you say you are...

....closer to Jesus
....not so close
....about the same as you were this time last year?

■STOP■

What does God have to say about getting close to Jesus?

- ■ Read the Bible passages.
- ■ Mark any discoveries you make.
- ■ Jot down any questions you are left with.
- ■ Talk about your discoveries and questions with the group.....

►PLAY►

In these two Bible passages Jesus says how important it is that we stay close to him.

As Jesus and his disciples went on their way, he came to a village where a woman named Martha welcomed him in her home. She had a sister named Mary, who sat down at the feet of the Lord and listened to his teaching. Martha was upset over all the work she had to do, so she came and said, 'Lord, don't you care that my sister has left me to do all the work by myself? Tell her to come and help me!'

The Lord answered her, 'Martha, Martha! You are worried and troubled over so many things, but just one is needed. Mary has chosen the right thing, and it will not be taken away from her.'

Luke 10:38– 42

What was the 'right thing' that Mary had chosen?

Did Jesus say that Martha was wrong to care about her housework?

What sort of 'fruit' does Jesus expect us to produce?

Another time, Jesus said this to his disciples....

'**I** am the vine, and you are the branches. Whoever remains in me, and I in him, will bear much fruit; for you can do nothing without me. Whoever does not remain in me is thrown out like a branch and dries up; such branches are gathered up and thrown into the fire, where they are burnt. If you remain in me and my words remain in you, then you will ask for anything you wish, and you shall have it. My Father's glory is shown by your bearing much fruit; and in this way you become my disciples. I love you just as the Father loves me; remain in my love. If you obey my commands, you will remain in my love, just as I have obeyed my Father's commands and remain in his love.'

John 15:5–10

> **vine,** n. A short tree that produces grapes. It has very long inter-twining branches. In the area where Jesus lived vines were very common.

Does this mean we can have anything we like just by asking God for it?

What does it mean to 'remain in Jesus' love'? What happens to people who don't?

FAST FORWARD

SOLO Martha was too busy with her housework to listen to Jesus. Draw something here that could distract you from listening to Jesus.

TWOS Thinking back to the Bible passages you have read, what advice would you give to these Christians? Choose one or two, then share your answers with the group.

I want to be a better Christian.

I'm a new Christian and I want to get to know Jesus.

I'm tired of being a Christian. I want some time off.

SOLO Think of a question or problem that someone might have about getting close to Jesus. Write it in the empty bubble.

GROUP Listen to the questions or problems each person has thought of. Then get together and try to think of some helpful and encouraging advice that you could give in reply.

SOLO Think back to the Bible passages you read earlier. Now make yourself a three-point action plan, setting out how you plan to grow closer to Jesus in the coming year. You might want to use some of these Bible words as you write down your three points:

| Obey • Remain • Listen • Ask |
| Love • Fruit |

1 ....

....

2 ....

....

3 ....

....

IIPAUSEII

WHAT WILL YOU DO?

Jason is planning to take a morning off school to help an old lady decorate her house. He asks the headteacher for permission, but she says he must come to school. Jason decides he will do it anyway, and asks you to say that he was ill. 'After all', he says, 'it's a good cause. So it's only a white lie.' The headteacher asks you where Jason is. What will you do?

Either spend a bit of time in silence while everyone in the group prays for themselves using the outline below,
or pray together, using the suggestions below as a guide.

Decide as a group which option you want to choose.

Thank God that he has accepted you and that he loves you.

Tell God you are sorry for the times when you have moved away from him or not listened to him.

Ask God to help you to grow closer to Jesus over the coming year.

Pray for the other members of the group, that they will grow closer to Jesus too.

TOUGH TALKING

If you want to be a Christian, do you have to read the Bible every day? How could you help someone who finds reading hard?

Is it OK for a Christian to go out with a non-Christian? Does this stop the Christian from keeping close to Jesus or help the non-Christian to get close to Jesus?

GOING FURTHER

If you want to think more about staying close to Jesus, check out these Bible passages :
1 Corinthians 6:19–20 — Bought by God
Psalms 16 and 23 — God is very close
Luke 14:25–33 — The cost of following Jesus

How can the

LOAD

Dave looked at the shopping list with a confident gleam in his eye. He hated it when his parents sent him to the shops, because he nearly always forgot something. It wasn't his fault either. He'd get distracted by something, or else he'd hear the clink of money in his pocket and forget it wasn't his. Then he'd buy some magazines or a record before he realised there wasn't enough left to get all the shopping. But whatever caused it, the result was always the same – a good shouting from Mum or Dad, perhaps even a clip round the ear, and any money he'd spent was taken from his paper-round money.

This time it was alright though. This time he was determined to get it right. He had a proper shopping list....he had the money all tied up in a hanky – shame he hadn't been able to find a clean one – and just to make sure, he was going to ask Sally to go with him. He dialled her number....no reply. Ah well, perhaps he'd try Sean. No good. Too busy. So he rang Marcus. Same answer....too much homework. Three phone calls later he gave up. He tucked the money into his jacket pocket and set off by himself.

'Who needs help?' he thought, as he strolled up to the check-out with a trolley full of stuff. He'd got the list, he'd done the shopping, and the money was in his jacket.....'Oh no !'
His confidence disappeared faster than a Mars bar at breakfast. The jacket? Still on the bus !

TWOS What Dave needs most is.....
(Tick one or add your own answer.)

A new jacket ☐
A good clip round the earhole ☐
Someone to do the shopping for him ☐
Someone to do the shopping with him ☐

Other...

GROUP Think of a time when you asked someone to help you do something you couldn't manage alone. Tell the group about it.

Has anyone in the group ever asked God to help them when they were finding something difficult? If so, what happened? Tell the group about it.

SOLO What telephone numbers do you use the most?

Think back over the past week or so and list some of the calls you have made. Write down the numbers on the lines below. If you can't remember the number just write the name.

....

....

....

Holy Spirit help me?

....

....

Why did you call these numbers?

SOLO Who would you call on for help if you were faced with the following situations? (Write down their name or number.)

You need money urgently but can't explain why

☎ ....

You have to make a vital decision about your future and you need advice

☎ ....

You need a shoulder to cry on

☎ ....

You have a problem about being a Christian and you need someone to talk it through with

☎ ....

You have to go shopping and you need some company

☎ ....

It's 2am and you're in serious trouble

☎ ....

TWOS Jesus described God's Holy Spirit as 'The Helper'.
Which of these pictures do you think comes closest to describing *your* picture of God's Holy Spirit?

A teacher

A spy

A sculptor

A ghost

...or can you think of a better picture of your own?

GROUP Can you think of any situations in which God's Holy Spirit has 'helped' members of your group? Tell each other about them.

In what ways did Jesus help his disciples? What things would they miss about him when he went away?

STOP

What does God have to say about the Holy Spirit?

- Read the Bible passages.
- Mark any discoveries you make.
- Jot down any questions you are left with.
- Talk about your discoveries and questions with the group.....

Why do you think some people find it hard to believe in the Holy Spirit?

PLAY

A few days before he died, Jesus told his disciples about the Holy Spirit who was going to come to them.

'I WILL ask the Father, and he will give you another Helper, who will stay with you forever. He is the Spirit who reveals the truth about God. The world cannot receive him, because it cannot see him or know him. But you know him, because he remains with you and is in you.

'The Helper, the Holy Spirit, whom the Father will send in my name, will teach you everything and make you remember all that I have told you.'

John 14:16–17, 26

Put a ring around every word that describes what the Holy Spirit can do for us.

How do you think the disciples would have felt when they heard this?

Paul told the Christians in Galatia some more things that the Holy Spirit would do for them....

WHAT I say is this: let the Spirit direct your lives, and you will not satisfy the desires of the human nature. For what our human nature wants is opposed to what the Spirit wants, and what the Spirit wants is opposed to what our human nature wants. These two are enemies, and this means that you cannot do what you want to do.....

But the Spirit produces love, joy, peace, patience, kindness, goodness, faithfulness, humility, and self-control. There is no law against such things as these. And those who belong to Christ Jesus have put to death their human nature with all its passions and desires. The Spirit has given us life; he must also control our lives.

Galatians 5:16–17, 22–25

Does this mean we should never do anything we enjoy?

'The world' is Jesus' way of talking about people who don't know God.

Paul says we should let the Spirit control our lives; but he also says that the Spirit produces self-control. So who should control our lives... us or the spirit?

FASE FORWARD

Look back to the Bible passages, and the words you have ringed. Choose one of the words from the passages to complete each of these sentences.

The Holy Spirit will ....with us, so we will never be alone.

The Holy Spirit will ....us, so we will know the truth about God.

If we let the Holy Spirit ....us, our human nature will not get the better of us.

Finish these two sentences. Choose from the list which follows or use your own words.

Doing what our human nature wants sounds...

....

Doing what the Spirit wants sounds

....

Exciting • Boring • Scary • Stupid
Sensible • Impossible • Limiting • Good

The results of the Holy Spirit's work in our lives are sometimes called 'the fruit' of the Spirit. How would you rate yourself on each part of the fruit that Paul mentions?

(Ring one apple on each row.) For each other person, think of one quality that the Holy Spirit is producing in them. Go and tell them what 'fruit' you can see in them.

	Useless		Half-way there		Perfect
Love					
Joy					
Peace					
Patience					
Kindness					
Goodness					
Faithfulness					
Humility					
Self-control					

WHAT WILL YOU DO?

A friend is interested in becoming a Christian. She says, 'I can believe in a Father God who created the world, and I can believe in Jesus who lived on earth, but this Holy Spirit stuff isn't really necessary, is it?' What will you do?

TOUGH TALKING

Some Christians believe that the Holy Spirit is given to everyone who follows Jesus. But other Christians believe that the Holy Spirit is something extra, that you have to ask for and receive after you've become a Christian. What do you think the Bible says?

If the Holy Spirit is there to teach us 'the truth about God', why do we need books, ministers, Bible study notes, this book etc?

IIPAUSEII

In many churches a candle is lit to remind people that God's presence, in the form of the Holy Spirit, is with them. Sit in a circle around a lighted candle. As you sit quietly looking at the flame, one person reads :

Holy Spirit, you are always with us.
Like a fire you give us light to see things clearly;
Like a fire you keep us warm in a cold world;
Like a fire you protect us from danger;
Like a fire you burn away all that displeases God.

In silence keep looking at the candle, and ask the Holy Spirit to work in you to produce his 'fruit' in your life.

Quietly sing a song about Holy Spirit together, such as 'Spirit of the living God, fall afresh on me', 'Spirit of God, unseen as the wind', or 'Breathe on me, breath of God'.

GOING FURTHER

If you want to think more about the Holy Spirit, check out these Bible passages :

Joel 2:28–32 – God promises his Holy Spirit
Acts 2:1–21 – God sends his Holy Spirit
1 Corinthians 12,13

–Gifts from the Holy Spirit

Is your group a Holy Huddle? Do the same faces appear week after week? Are you becoming inward-looking?

Perhaps you should....

PREPARE TO SHARE!

Many people ask questions about life and faith while they are teenagers. And many of your friends could find a living faith in the Lord Jesus – if your group plays its part.

Here are some points to think about as you prepare to share :

◆ As a Christian you need to understand your faith clearly. How else can you give a clear account of it to other people?

◆ Sharing the love of God is part of the ongoing work of the youth group. It's not a matter of words, but of loving caring action. So don't just wait for a special time such as a mission or evangelistic event.

◆ Your own friends and work-mates are the mission field God has given you. Think about how you can share the good news of Jesus with them first.

STEVE Taylor and the youth group from Chester-le-Street, County Durham, held a week's Youth Festival. They took over the old council offices and turned them into a coffee bar, with music, drama, food and chat all week long. At the same time, groups of young people and invited guests visited local schools, took assemblies, did street theatre and talked about Jesus. By the end of the week the whole town seemed to have got the message that Jesus is good news.

We asked Steve for some tips on....

PLANNING AN EVANGELISTIC EVENT

❝Good news!
AN evangelistic event should be great fun. The task is a very serious one, but the message is good news. If you're going to have a service, make it a festival! If you're going to have a meeting, make it a celebration! Some groups are able to organise regular evangelistic activities, such as a coffee bar, a non-alcoholic pub or a monthly guest night. But **I would like every group to think about organising an evangelistic event at least once a year. It could take all sorts of forms, but it must be something that you would be happy to invite your friends to....**an opportunity to tell them the good news about Jesus.

IDEAS IDEAS IDEAS IDEAS

BE imaginative. Try to think what sort of event will help you to communicate the message to your friends. Tell the story of what God has done for you. The difference Christ has made in your life will be challenging to your friends. You could involve others outside your group who have particular talents, or you could make it a home-grown event. Try to make sure that every person in your group has a part to play and an opportunity to share.

DON'T FORGET DON'T FORGET

▼ Make sure you pray regularly for the event and share news with the rest of your church.

▼ Be prepared to change your plans in the light of your prayers and comments from others.

▼ Set yourself some goals. How many new young Christians can your group take on board? How many can you nurture properly?

▼ Prepare a budget and work out where the money will come from.

▼ Very soon after the event there should be some basic Christian teaching for new believers and people who are just interested.

Step 1
When your friends see or hear about your group, do they see a lively and loving group, or a boring and bitchy group ?

Step 2
Can you give a short, clear presentation of the good news? Or do you need some more practice?

Step 3
Is your group the sort of group where newcomers are made welcome and helped to grow as Christians? If not, what can you do about it ?

WHY NOT?

◆ ...use these pages to help you think about using your group as a base for evangelism.

◆ ....practise talking about what you believe and what God has done for you. You could get into pairs and practise on each other.

◆ ....pray regularly for one friend who is not yet a Christian.

◆ ....plan an evangelistic event together, using Steve's tips to help you.

How can I know

LOAD

Sam looked along the shelves of glossy brochures in the Careers Room. There were far too many. How could she possibly decide what to do next?

Her science teacher said she should stay on at school and do A levels – that's if her GCSE results were OK. But she'd read something in a magazine that seemed to say it was better to go off to college, rather than stay at the same school.

On the other hand, she didn't really know if she wanted to do more exams. Dad said it was time she went out to work. Perhaps she should. Most of her friends had got jobs and she was afraid she might get left behind.

Just at the moment there was only one thing she wanted to do. Bury her head in the sand.

Just then Mike breezed in. 'Hi Sam! Made up your mind yet?' Sam shook her head.

'I have! I'm going on the "Give-a-Year" scheme. God's called me into full–time work for him.'

'Oh,' said Sam. She didn't really know what to say. She wished God would call her to do something, but she wasn't really sure what getting called meant. Before she could ask, Mike said....

'Oh well, keep on praying. I'm sure he'll guide you soon.'

'I hope so,' Sam thought, as she picked up yet another free pamphlet. 'I really do.'

God's plan for me?

 What advice would you give to Sam? How should she decide what to do? (Tick one or more, or add your own answer.)

Close her eyes and pick out a brochure ❏
Talk to a Christian friend or minister ❏
Read the Bible and look for an answer ❏
Go to a fortune teller and ask what to do ❏
Ask for advice from a teacher ❏
Pray about the decision and wait for
    God to answer ❏
Do whatever seems most sensible ❏

Other ....

Tell the group which answer(s) you have chosen, and why.

 Think back to an important decision you have recently had to make. How did you decide what you should do? In what way, if any, was God involved in your decision? Tell the group about it.

 Mike said God had 'called' him to work on the 'Give-a-Year' scheme. What do you think he might have meant by that?

 Fill in the gaps in these sentences using the words 'always', 'sometimes' or 'never'.

It is .... easy to know what God wants us to do.

It is .... easy to do what God wants us to do.

What God wants is .... the same as what we want.

Do you think God has an exact plan for each of our lives? For instance, do you think God has one particular job in mind for Sam, or are there lots of things she could do which would be equally OK?

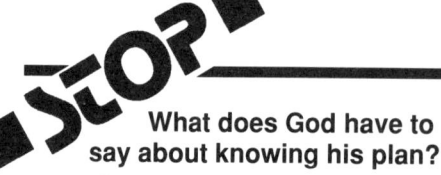

What sort of people does God lead and guide?

STOP

What does God have to say about knowing his plan?

- Read the Bible passages.
- Mark any discoveries you make.
- Jot down any questions you are left with.
- Talk about your discoveries and questions with the group.....

PLAY

This passage is part of a Psalm. The writer is asking God to guide him and protect him.

B ECAUSE the LORD is
righteous and good,
   he teaches sinners the path
      they should follow.
He leads the humble in the
   right way
   and teaches them his will.
With faithfulness and love he
   leads
   all who keep his covenant
      and obey his commands.

Keep your promise, LORD, and
   forgive my sins,
   for they are many.
Those who have reverence for
   the LORD
   will learn from him the
      path they should follow.

Psalm 25:8–12

What promise?

What is this person's attitude to God?

What does Paul mean when he says that God has shown us 'great mercy'?

Paul wrote this in a letter to the Christians in Rome. He wanted them to know how to follow God's plan for them.

S o then, my brothers, because of God's great mercy to us I appeal to you: offer yourselves as a living sacrifice to God, dedicated to his service and pleasing to him. This is the true worship that you should offer. Do not conform yourselves to the standards of this world, but let God transform you inwardly by a complete change of your mind. Then you will be able to know the will of God – what is good and is pleasing to him and is perfect.

Romans 12:1–2

What does this mean? Does it mean we have to die?

How can we know what God's will for us is?

FAST FORWARD

Here are some ways that people make important decisions. How highly do you rate each one as a way of finding out God's plan for you? Give them points from 1–10 where 1 is 'useless' and 10 is 'very good'.

Use a bit of common sense .....
Spin a coin .....
Follow your inner feelings .....
Open the Bible at random and
    read a verse .....
Ask advice from a friend .....
Do what you really want to .....
Ask God for help and wait for an answer .....

Other ....

 Mark an ✗ somewhere on each of these lines.

Since I became a Christian I have been....

| completely transformed | the same as ever |

When I hear that God wants to transform me completely my reaction is.....

| No thanks | Yes please |

When it comes to knowing God's plan for my life....

| I'm the local expert | I haven't a clue |

 Are there any areas of your life that still need to be 'offered to God', or placed under his control? Make a private note of them here.

1 ....

2 ....

3 ....

How can you give God control of these areas of your life?

Imagine that the members of your group were lost together up a misty mountain a long way from home. Talk together and decide what action you would take. Think of something that each person could contribute to help you in that situation.

WHAT WILL YOU DO?

A friend of yours has an important decision to make about which course to take at school or college. He asks you to tell him what to do. What will you do?

TOUGH TALKING

Why do you think so many people go to fortune tellers and clairvoyants, or read their horoscopes? Can God ever speak through them?

If we go away from God's plan for us, is it possible to get back onto it? Does God have a 'plan B' for our lives in case 'plan A' fails?

‖PAUSE‖

As a group, write a prayer or a song in two parts. In the first part, thank God for the times he has guided you and led you in the past. In the second part ask him to show you his plan for you in the future. Tell him that you trust him to take care of you.

When you have written your prayer or song, keep a time of silence, then say or sing it together.

If your prayer or song is good, why not offer it to your church to use in their worship, or to your school for use at assembly?

GOING FURTHER

If you want to know more about how to follow God's plan for your life check out these Bible passages :

Joshua 1:1–18

– God tells Joshua what to do

John 14:1–14 – Jesus is our guide

Acts 16:6–10 – God guides Paul

What does the

LOAD

Kelvin was being his usual cheery self.

'Gets you down, doesn't it?' he observed to the rest of the group propping up the outside wall of the biology lab.

'What's that then Kel?' asked Parmjit.

'All these wars an' that an' AIDS'

'Yeah! An' unemployment an' crime an' famines,' added Ravi.

'Yeah! An pollution an' the ozone layer an' the whales an' all,' continued Kelvin. 'I mean let's face it, the world could be blown to bits right now.'

'Lucky escape if it was!' Sandra broke in glumly. 'I've got a maths test next period, and I'm nowhere near ready for it.'

They all slumped back against the wall.

'What's the matter with you then, Tom? What are you looking so happy for?' demanded Kelvin as he pushed Tom's wheelchair towards the maths room. He was angry that anyone else could be smiling when he was feeling so cheesed off. 'Doesn't anything get you down?'

'Only one thing.' They were all interested. Tom never got down.

'What's that then?'

'You lot moaning all the time!'

future hold?

 SOLO Put an ✗ on the line to show who you think you are most like.

Kelvin   *Tom*

 TWOS Compare your answer with your partner's. Then ask if they would put *your* ✗ in the same place as you did.

 GROUP Take a vote in your group to decide which of these factors is most likely to wipe out life on earth.

Conventional war	.....
Nuclear war	.....
AIDS	.....
Other diseases	.....
Maths tests	.....
Unemployment	.....
Famine	.....
Politicians	.....
Pollution	.....
Crime	.....
Moaning	.....
Business people	.....
Greed	.....
Ordinary people	.....
Invaders from another planet	.....
God	.....

 GROUP Take another vote to see how long most people think life on this earth will last.

Up to 10 years	.....
Up to 20 years	.....
Up to 50 years	.....
Up to 100 years	.....
Up to 1000 years	.....
Millions of years	.....

 SOLO Draw your face here to show how all this voting and discussion makes you feel.

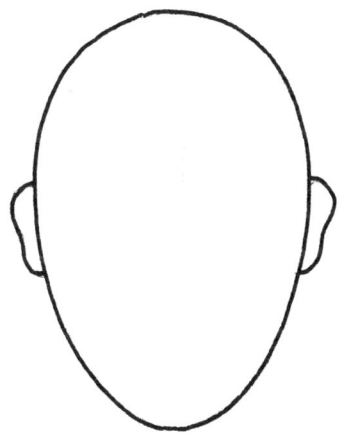

■STOP■

What does God have to say about the future of the world?

■ Read the Bible passages.
■ Mark any discoveries you make.
■ Jot down any questions you are left with.
■ Talk about your discoveries and questions with the group.....

Who are 'his chosen people'? Who will be gathered together by the angels, and who will be left behind?

►PLAY►

In this passage from Matthew's gospel, Jesus tells his disciples that one day he will return to the earth.

How will Jesus' second appearance on earth be different from his first?

Why?

T HEN the sign of the Son of Man will appear in the sky; and all the peoples of earth will weep as they see the Son of Man coming on the clouds of heaven with power and great glory. The great trumpet will sound, and he will send out his angels to the four corners of the earth, and they will gather his chosen people from one end of the world to the other....

....That is how it will be when the Son of Man comes. At that time two men will be working in a field: one will be taken away, the other will be left behind. Two women will be at a mill grinding meal: one will be taken away, the other will be left behind. Be on your guard, then, because you do not know what day your Lord will come. If the owner of a house knew the time when the thief would come, you can be sure that he would stay awake and not let the thief break into his house. So then, you must always be ready, because the Son of Man will come at an hour when you are not expecting him.

Matthew 24:30–31, 39b–44

What will it be like when God's people meet him face to face?

THEN I saw a new heaven and a new earth. The first heaven and the first earth disappeared, and the sea vanished. And I saw the Holy City, the new Jerusalem, coming down out of heaven from God, prepared and ready, like a bride dressed to meet her husband. I heard a loud voice speaking from the throne: 'Now God's home is with mankind! He will live with them, and they shall be his people. God himself will be with them, and he will be their God. He will wipe away all tears from their eyes. There will be no more death, no more grief or crying or pain. The old things have disappeared.'

Then the one who sits on the throne said, 'And now I make all things new!' He also said to me, 'Write this, because these words are true and can be trusted.'

Revelation 21:1–5

This passage is part of a vision or 'revelation' in which God showed John what will happen when the world ends.

This is picture language for God's people together in heaven.

'Son of Man': Jesus' name for himself

What do you hope will have disappeared? What would you like God to make new?

How do we know these words can be trusted?

FAST FORWARD

Jesus said we should 'always be ready' for the day when he returns. What do you think this means? (Tick one or more, or add your own answer.)

TWOS

Have a bag packed so you're ready to leave ❑

Live as if he was coming back today ❑

Don't get too attached to things in this world ❑

Buy him a 'welcome back' present ❑

Don't do anything you wouldn't want Jesus to see ❑

Other ....

SOLO Mark an **X** on the lines somewhere between the two extremes.

When I think about Jesus returning to the earth I want to say....

Oh no! _____ *Yippee!*

If Jesus came back today I would be....

Ready _____ *Caught*
and waiting *unprepared*

TWOS Think of a book, film or song title to describe how you see the future of the world, eg 'Great Expectations', 'A Comedy of Errors', 'Neighbours', 'Help!'.

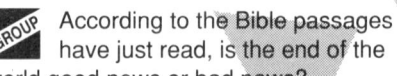

GROUP According to the Bible passages you have just read, is the end of the world good news or bad news?

GROUP As you come to the end of this book, think together about the next stage in the life of this group. How can you help each other to get ready for Jesus' return? What is the next step for you? Work at another book together? Get to know each other socially? Get involved in some practical caring project? Learn how to worship God together? Or what?

||PAUSE||

WHAT WILL YOU DO?

Think back to the story in the LOAD section. Imagine that you are with Kelvin and the others getting depressed about the state of the world. What will you do?

TOUGH TALKING

If God is loving and merciful, how come the Bible says some people will be left behind when Jesus takes his followers to heaven? Won't he find a way of including everybody?

Some people believe that human beings will destroy the world with nuclear weapons. Others believe that we need them to keep people from fighting. What do you think?

GOING FURTHER

If you want to think more about Jesus' second coming and the end of the world, check out these Bible passages:

Acts 1:6–11   – *Jesus will return*

Matthew 25:1–13   –*A warning*

1 Thessalonians 4:13–5:11 – Be prepared

Ready rap!
One person chants the alternate lines of this rap, and the whole group responds with 'Let's get ready'. You can add your own lines in the middle. Give yourselves a rhythm by clapping your hands or clicking your fingers. Or you could use pots and pans or keys for a really good rhythm!

Jesus is coming
Let's get ready
Maybe this year
Let's get ready
Maybe ten years
Let's get ready
Maybe thousands
Let's get ready
Are you preparing?
Let's get ready
Gonna be a party
Let's get ready
You're invited
Let's get ready
Will you be ready?
Let's get ready
Don't disappoint him
Let's get ready
Let's get ready
Let's get ready, Yeah!

How to use

This book has two aims....

■ To help you hear what God has to say to you

Of course there's no point in just hearing God speak for the sake of it. When God speaks to us he always wants us to change. So you need to decide how you will put what you hear into practice too.

■ To help you grow together as a group

The Christian life is for living together. That means getting to know each other, sharing ideas, encouraging each other and challenging each other to follow Jesus.

Here's how it works....

Each track in this book is divided into four sections :

LOAD This is the section to get you started. It's a chance for all the members of the group to share their ideas and experiences. Ask someone to read the scene-setter story aloud to the rest of the group. Then work through the questions that follow. You should work by yourselves, in pairs or all together as indicated by the symbols beside the questions. But try to work through the questions at the same pace so that no one gets left behind. Every member of your group is special. So make sure that everyone gets a chance to contribute.

PLAY The aim of this section is to find out what God has to say to you

through his Word, the Bible.

You can either get together on this section or work individually. *Read through the Bible passages with a pencil in your hand. If anything strikes you as interesting, make a note of it in the book.* If there's anything you don't understand, or any questions you'd like answered, write them in too. We've pencilled in a few questions that occurred to us, but you can add your own.

When you've had a chance to work through the Bible passages and scribbled down your comments and questions, *get together with the rest of the group and talk through the questions you have raised, and the ones we thought of.* If there are too many questions to work through, choose the most important ones, or save some for another session. See if you can work out what God is saying through the Bible.

FAST FORWARD This is where the action starts. What are you going to do about the things that God is saying to you? Work through these questions as you did before. The *Fast forward* section always gives an opportunity for the members of the group to encourage and affirm one another, to share discoveries and to make plans.

What will you do? is a test of how much you have changed in the light of what you think God is saying. When it comes to the crunch what will you do? Decide for yourself then share your answer with the group. Be honest!

Tough talking is an optional section, mostly for older groups who like to struggle with hard questions. There are no easy answers here.

this book....

Going further is another optional section. It is not intended for you to use in the group session, but you may want to read through these passages in the week after the meeting to understand the subject even better. And they may help you with some of the *Tough talking* questions.

IIPAUSEII   At the end of each track, take a *Pause* and spend some time focussing on God. Some groups will want to sing together or have a time of open prayer. If your group is not used to worship and praying together start with a few of the simpler ideas.

Making it work ...

Getting going
Every group meeting should start with a fun time to help everyone to relax together. This is particularly important if the members of the group don't know each other very well, or if there are new members. Ideas for breaking the ice are contained in the *Meeting points* section of the book. Pick on one or two of these ideas and enjoy them together. Don't be tempted to miss out this important warm-up stage of the group's meeting.

So much to do....so little time!
Different groups have different amounts of time available. Each track contains at least enough material for a whole evening together. Many groups won't be able to manage all the material at a single sitting. Don't worry! Either split the material over two or more sessions, or else select a couple of exercises from each section. It is much better to cover a few questions well than to try to do everything quickly. If one question seems particularly interesting or important for your group, spend longer on it. If there's a question that doesn't apply so much to you, just skip it.

Who's in charge?
Every group needs a leader. But it doesn't necessarily have to be the same person all the time. This book is designed so that group members could take it in turns to lead sessions. This is good experience, and it can also help to build the group if everyone agrees to co-operate with the session leader.

Here are some do's and don'ts for people leading a group session....

....do prepare!
Look through the material before the meeting. Decide what *Meeting points* you will use. Think about how long you want to spend on each section. Look carefully at the Bible passages and look up anything you think people may not understand. It may help if you have looked through the *Going further* passages too.

....don't panic!
The group leader doesn't have to know all the answers. If there are things that you don't know or questions that you can't answer, that's OK! It might be helpful to have a Bible commentary or handbook available so that you can check out any tricky questions. And you can always make a note to ask someone for help and report back to the group.

....do make sure everyone has a chance to contribute.
The leader will need to make sure that quieter people are able to join in the group discussions as well as more noisy ones. The leader will also make sure that it's not always the same people who are asked to share their answers or read out the stories.

....don't dominate!
The group belongs to everyone and everyone should be able to contribute. It's your job to make sure they can. Don't allow the group to be dominated by one person....especially if that person is yourself! If you are an adult leader of a teenage group you will need to be particularly careful to make sure that everyone is allowed to make their own discoveries and move at their own pace.

....do keep things moving.
It's your job to get the group together at the start of the session, and to decide how long to spend on each section. Gently make sure that everyone knows where the session is going. 'I think it's time we moved on now.' 'We'll have two minutes in pairs now, then we'll come together to discuss our answers.' 'Does anyone mind if we skip this next question?'

Notes for each track

Theme
The tracks in this book are about living life in partnership with God. Introduce this theme to your group before you begin the book.

Here are some notes to help you plan for each group meeting.

Track 1
What's most important to me?
This track will introduce your group members to Serendipity, and help them to work out where they are when it comes to following Jesus. In particular, group members are asked to think about anything that is getting in the way of their following him.

If your group don't know each other particularly well why not play 'The hello game' from the *Meeting points* section.

Load This section is mostly for fun, although the last two questions have a serious point. What are the things that your group members really value highly? They don't have to be 'things' like chocolate. They could be people, or ambitions, or something else. Ask people to share their answers if they want to, but never force anyone to say what they have written.

Play Make sure you have read the notes in the 'How to use this book' section. Give the group about ten minutes to read through the Bible passages with a pencil in one hand, marking anything interesting and adding any questions they may have. Then read the passages together, and talk through some of the points that have been raised.

Fast forward You may have to help group members to think of ways in which they might answer the first question. Decide carefully whether the second question (which begins, 'the thought of giving up everything to follow Jesus ...') is right for your group to tackle at this point. At this stage in the book it is important that every group member knows that they can be honest and that no one will look down on them for their feelings. If you do use this question, decide how you will help someone for whom the thought of giving up everything to follow Jesus does not seem to be good news. For some people the next step will be to take an experimental step of faith, whilst others will need more thinking time. You could suggest these options.

Track 2
Who's in control?
Many people believe that the world is controlled by fate or sheer chance. Others believe that the world is in the grip of the Devil. This track shows that God is ultimately in control, even if the Devil has some temporary power. Be ready to help or counsel people who have had occult experience. You may need the help of a more experienced Christian.

Play You may want to fill in some more details from the story of Job. The Good News Bible has an introduction to Job which could be useful.

Fast forward You could go deeper in looking at 'who's in control of the world?' by discussing why people sometimes think the false answers are true.

Pause Some groups find praying together very difficult. Can you think of a simple way to help people who are not used to prayer? It sometimes helps for people to write down a few words or ideas before praying in a group. Of course no one should feel they are under pressure to pray out loud. If you are going to pray together you should make it clear that silence is OK.

If a bit more noise is called for, why not have some fun with the do-it-yourself rap!

Track 3
How can I get closer to Jesus?
Being a Christian is not a once-for-all decision. It is a continual process of getting closer to Jesus. And that is the subject of this track.

Play Show the group a picture of a vine if you can, and talk with them about what Jesus might have meant by using this image of our relationship with him.

If time is short you may need to omit (or do another time) the question about having anything we like just by asking God for it.

Tough talking Be aware that the question of Christians and non-Christians going out is a very sensitive one for many teenagers. It is not usually helpful to be too dogmatic about this.

Track 4
How can the Holy Spirit help me?
This track is about the Holy Spirit's work in our lives. We concentrate on his role as a helper and companion.

Load If you are short of time, miss out the two questions about telephone numbers.

Play Read through the passages before the session and ring all the appropriate words to make sure that no important truths are missed out.

Track 5
How can I know God's plan for me?
This track is about the ways God guides us. Many young people are confused about this. Guidance is not a guessing game, and there is nothing 'magical' about finding God's plan. It has a lot to do with 'godly common sense'.

Load Many young people face the kind of choices that Sam is facing. But if your group is well below school leaving age perhaps they would be better able to understand the kind of decisions that are required in choosing subject options.

Encourage group members to share stories about the ways God has cared for them or guided them. Look for very small instances as well as ones that seem specially important.

Fast forward You could use the last question as a role-play. Make sure that each person is made to feel valued by having some definite contribution to make to the situation, be it making the tea, carrying the luggage or reading the map.

Pause Use a flip chart or several large sheets of paper to write up everyone's ideas for the song or prayer. Try to weave all the ideas together, so that no one's contribution is lost.

Track 6
What does the future hold?

This track is about the end of the world. The Bible tells us that the world as we know it will come to an end when Jesus returns. The important thing is not to ask when or how that will happen, though they are questions that interest many teenagers. What is important is that we live in readiness for Jesus' return.

Load Don't spend too long on this section. It is the least important part of this track.

Play Try to help your group understand that these passages use a lot of picture language to describe Jesus' return and the end of the world. A good commentary may help.

Fast forward Spend time on the first two questions and talk about them together.

Is there any way that you can ensure that all members of the group have a say in making plans for the future?

Keep in touch with Serendipity

Serendipity is more than just a brand name for this book of group meetings. We exist to provide all sorts of help for those who work with young people or adults: Bible study outlines, resource evenings, training for leaders of small groups. If you would like us to keep you posted with news of future books and events, cut out this box and send it to us.

NAME ....

ADDRESS ....

....

....

I am particularly interested in:

youth groups .... {tick as
adult groups .... {appropriate

Send to: Serendipity UK, 48 Peterborough Road, London SW6 3EB